What People Are Saying

AUTHORS

"I like what Sam Williamson has to say about how good people — people like us — may be piling burdens on our children they can't possibly bear. Has the good news of the gospel magically morphed into bad news for them? Read Sam's provocative new book to find out."   — Ann Spangler, Author, *Praying the Names of God* (and many other books)

"These days we hear so much and think so little. We consume without digesting and then wonder why our body is acting strangely. In this book, Sam helps us look carefully, graciously, and wonder-fully at the gospel and the beliefs of our heart."   — Gary Barkalow, founding director of The Noble Heart, and Author, *It's Your Call.*

"Sam Williamson is a bit of pot-stirrer. He makes you think, whether you want to or not. He takes stands, whether you agree with them or not. He wants to talk about the gospel, whether you've heard it a million times or not. Is it all simpler or more complicated than we think? Read what he says and decide for yourself."

—Joanne Beckman, Author, *Groceries on a Saturday Morning, Confession from Real-Life Christianity*

"I wish I would've read this when I was kid — long before I ever entered a Sunday school classroom as a jaded teenager. I might not have left the church at an early age. I'm grateful, though, that I'll have it to introduce my son to a different way of living out his faith."

—Jeff Goins, Author, *The In-Between*

READERS

"This book is a must-read for every Christian, whether they are a new convert or a seasoned saint! … I cannot recommend this book highly enough!"   —*Michelle*

"This is the most brilliant book I have read recently. I feel like I highlighted almost everything, because everything was wonderfully insightful and thought provoking."   —*Jolene*

"I have been trying to unravel the paradox of Grace for a long time. Sam does an awesome job of breaking it down into something I understand better than anything else I've read."   —*A. C.*

"Don't miss reading this eye opening book. Bring your own shovels and pickaxes because you will find yourself exploring within your own heart … You will live an adventure you will not forget, finding nuggets of gold along the way. You will become a treasure hunter through a path that will lead you to your very own pot of gold."   — *R. B.*

"I want a copy for everyone I see!"   — *Kassie*

"When I first saw this book, I missed the subtitle, 'How Moralism Suffocates Grace,' and thus almost missed one of the best books I've read in a l-o-n-g time."   — *A. R.*

"This is the best book I've read in a long time (and I read a lot of books)."   — *L. M.*

"This was as insightful view as I have ever read of God's grace and how simple it can be and the real freedom it can bring when we accept it."   — *Gentz*

"This is a GREAT book. I will be reading it over and over as it has a wealth of information. I like the mixture of stories and Scripture … You will not be disappointed in reading a very well written book you can use to teach."   — *Kenneth*

"I've read a lot of books on Christian living and sometimes you just scream "get to the point!" Sam says what he means quickly, in a style like talking to a friend on the front porch over a cup of coffee."   — *L. B.*

Is Sunday School
Destroying Our Kids?

How Moralism

Suffocates Grace

SAMUEL C. WILLIAMSON

http://beliefsoftheheart.com/
Sam@BeliefsoftheHeart.com

Unless otherwise indicated, all Scripture quotations are from *The Holy Bible, English Standard Version,* copyright ©2001 by Crossway Bibles, a division of Good News Publishers. Used by permission. All rights reserved.

Scripture quotations marked (NIV) are taken from the *Holy Bible, New International Version®, NIV®.* Copyright ©1973, 1978, 1984, 2011 by Biblica, Inc. Used by permission of Zondervan. All rights reserved worldwide. www.zondervan.com, The "NIV" and "New International Version" are trademarks registered in the United States Patent and Trademark Office by Biblica, Inc.™

The author's paraphrases and translations of Scripture are marked as (par).
Italics in Scripture quotations indicate emphasis added.

Editor: Robert Hartig (www.thecopyfox.com)
Cover Design: Beetiful Book Covers (bookcovers.beetiful.com)
Publishing Services: Sellbox.com

ISBN (paperback): 978-1-941024-00-3
ISBN (eBook): 978-1-941024-01-0

Second printing.

Acknowledgements

We are not alone. Every accomplishment we ever realize comes from the support of — and sometimes at the cost of — family and friends we love. I would like to thank the following people:

- My wife, Carla, who knows the good, the bad, and the ugly about me and still miraculously loves me. It's called grace.
- My kids and their wives, Sam and Michele, David and Sarah, Jonathan, and Rebekah. They have no delusions about their father and love him anyway.
- Special thanks to my son Jonathan who gave me hours of his time listening, cajoling, suggesting, and laughing.
- My parents, one living and one passed away. You first taught me grace.
- My friend Gary Barkalow, who helped me understand my calling. I know of no other person or ministry so equipped to help others understand theirs. http://thenobleheart.com/
- All my Sunday school teachers. They really did teach me the gospel, and they demonstrated it

weekly as they gracefully put up with my adolescent antics.

- My editor, Bob Hartig, who challenged, corrected, and encouraged me.
- Tim Keller, whose preaching and writing has taught me so much about the gospel, though I've never met him.

I owe you all a debt that I shall never be able to repay.

Contents

Preface

I once heard someone say, "I think like a genius, I speak like a Greek orator, but I write like an idiot." I thought, That's me! That was exactly how I felt.

Except for the genius and orator parts.

I grew up in a family that loved to read. Our bookshelves and coffee tables overflowed with well-worn books. Our month-long summer camping trips always included beer boxes full of books. My parents were teetotalers, but those boxes—designed for twenty-four longneck bottles—were the perfect size for our traveling library.

We spent those summer months sailing our small Sunfish sailboat and sipping spirits drawn from our beer-boxed books.

And ever since then, I wanted to be a writer. I loved books written by others, and I wanted to write one myself. I longed for the day when others would be caught up by the ideas and stories that I put to paper. I had just one problem: I really didn't like to write.

In college, I was forced to write scores of history and philosophy papers, but I didn't enjoy it. I was loosely interested in the topics, but I was mainly interested in completing my classes so I could finish college—so I wouldn't have to write anymore.

During my twenty-five years in business, I wrote several user manuals, dozens of marketing pieces, hundreds of business proposals, and thousands and thousands of emails. All of them had this in common: they were written by someone who hated to write.

BLOGGING

In 2008, I felt God call me to full-time ministry. I began by preaching in vacant pulpits, speaking at retreats, and talking one-on-one with guys. I was neither a genius nor a Greek orator, but no one threw tomatoes either.

I created a website (http://beliefsoftheheart.com/) and started blogging. My blogging life consisted of creating video blogs. I figured that contemporary culture prefers visuals, and I chose video because—well ...

I really hated to write.

I BECAME A TREASURE HUNTER

After months of video blogging, I was stumped by a topic that just didn't seem to work on video. After six or seven frustrating "takes," I wanted to take a tomato and throw it at that untalented on-screen talent, Me.

I decided to write out the blog just to tighten up the topic a bit. The more I wrote it, the more I enjoyed choosing the right words and nuancing the structure. Something amazing happened, maybe something miraculous.

I learned I loved to write.

But not just about anything. I loved writing as a tool for exploration. Writing became an adventure, and words and syntax became the shovels and pickaxes of a treasure hunter. I was most curious about our secret, hidden, and usually unexamined beliefs, those convictions that drive how we live.

BELIEFS OF THE HEART

Studying Intellectual History and trying to figure out software solutions for clients taught me something. I discovered that we all have buried, inarticulate desires. We say we want X, but that X is really the result of wanting something deeper, a secret longing for Y.

We also have hidden beliefs. We say we believe God loves us, yet we're angry, timid, anxious, and fearful. Our head says we know God loves us, but the deepest belief of our heart says we have to be really, really good or else God will reject us.

For every one of us, there is a desire beneath our desires, a sin beneath our sins, and a motivation beneath our motivations. We don't know the deepest beliefs of our heart.

Our most troubling problems arise from misunderstanding grace. We say we love grace, but I think we secretly dislike it. Christian culture claims to embrace grace—what's not to like? But the truth is that we only like parts of it, not the whole package.

And that is our problem.

BECAUSE GRACE IS AN ECOSYSTEM

Yellowstone Park was formed to preserve an incredibly beautiful and varied ecosystem. But early in the park's history, "bad" predators such as wolves were hunted to extinction. When the wolves were eliminated, the elk herds expanded exponentially, and the entire ecosystem—plants, landscape, and other animals—began to collapse.

Like Yellowstone, grace is an ecosystem with interdependent parts.[1] When Yellowstone got rid of its "bad" animals, the good animals began to die too. Similarly, when we rid grace of the parts we don't like, the good parts also die. Until we understand and embrace *all* of the interacting elements of grace, we won't live the joyful, rich life that it promises.

Grace means that we were so broken—the Puritan preachers said we are so wicked!—that the only cure was the death of God's Son. But we are also so loved that Jesus suffered willingly on our behalf.

Some preachers like the "we are so wicked" part, but they are silent about the love part. Their messages leave us condemned, insecure, constantly striving, and joy-less. We never know if our hard work is good enough. Because it isn't.

Other preachers like the "we are so loved" part, but they are quiet about our sins. Those messages don't seem to change us either. Of course we're loved. We're good people. I'm okay and you're okay. But that love hasn't electrified us. We're still angry and anxious.

THE PACKAGE DEAL

Grace means we are both unworthy of God's love yet profoundly loved by him nevertheless, both at the same time. When we know our unworthiness, and when we also know that we are loved just because we are loved, something amazing happens: the wonder of grace ex-plodes in our hearts into the real joy we've always want-ed.

That's why John Newton—a man who once bought and sold slaves—could write his famous hymn, "Amaz-ing Grace." He knew his unworthiness, but at the same time, he also knew the richness of God's love. His expe-rience of the full package of grace is what gave birth to the song that has touched the hearts of millions.

I hope that a meditation on the whole ecosystem of God's grace will likewise cause a chain-reaction, a nuclear explosion of joy in your heart. It's the only joy that will finally empower you and me to live the lives we were designed for—lives of joy and love.

>Sam
>
>Ann Arbor, Michigan
>
>November 2013

Chapter 1
Is Sunday School Destroying Our Kids?

The main thing we learn from a serious attempt to practice the Christian virtues is that we fail. If there was any idea that God had set us a sort of exam and that we might get good marks by deserving them, that has to be wiped out. — C. S. Lewis

Several years ago I met with a woman distraught over her son's rejection of Christianity.

She said, "I did everything I could to raise him right. I taught him to be like the 'heroes of faith,' with the faithfulness of Abraham, the goodness of Joseph, the pure heart of David, and the obedience of Esther."

She wondered why he had rejected Christianity.

I wondered why it took him so long.

HERE IS HOW WE DESTROY
THE GOSPEL MESSAGE

Look at almost any Sunday school curriculum and you'll find the following:

- Abraham was faithful, and God made him the father of a nation. *So be faithful like Abraham.*
- Joseph was a good little boy (unlike his "bad" brothers), and God made him prime minister of Egypt. *So be good like Joseph.*
- David had a pure heart (unlike his brothers), and God made him king of Israel. *So have a pure heart like David.*
- Esther was an obedient girl. God made her queen of Persia, and she saved God's people. *So be obedient like Esther.*
- Finally, if we fail to be good, Jesus will forgive us. (This comes as a PS tacked onto the end.)

What's so bad about these Sunday school lessons?

Nothing really. Except that they lie about God, they lie about these "heroes of the faith," they lie about the Bible, and they lie about the gospel. Oh, and they create "younger brother" rebels and "older brother" Pharisees. Apart from that, they are pretty good.

Is the gospel our central theme, or is it a PS tacked onto the end?

THE GOSPEL IS MORE THAN GOOD MORALS

Morality is good, desirable, lacking to some degree in all of us, and probably not preached enough from the pulpit. We need moral people. In a world where darkness expresses itself in everything from petty theft to genocide, healthy morals enable us to peacefully coexist. And that is good. Essential, even. It just isn't the gospel.

In his appendix to *The Abolition of Man,* C. S. Lewis shows how all the major religious thinkers share similar moral values. He quotes from ancient Egyptian, Babylonian, Confucian, Hindu, Norse, Greek, Native American, Roman, and Jewish writings. Despite the wide gulfs of geography, time, and culture, there is an amazing consistency in moral wisdom concerning fidelity, honesty, beneficence, duties, mercy, and justice.

And that is the point: Most religions believe in mostly the same moralities. So what distinguishes Christianity?

Morality is greatly to be desired, but it's just morality. Preaching moral performance isn't why Jesus came. He came to free us from the *power* of sin, not just the actions of sin; he came to bring us a supernatural change in our hearts, a rebirth.

We need the gospel. And the gospel exceeds mere morality.

THE GOSPEL STORYLINE

The message of the gospel—the entire storyline of Scripture—is God's loving pursuit of people who run from him as fast as they can and who live lives unworthy of his love.

That's why it's called *grace*.

But our Sunday school lessons teach us to be good little boys and girls, and if we are, then God will love us and use us. It's the total opposite of the gospel. It's a counterfeit of the worst kind.

THE INSIDE OUT OF THE GOSPEL

The wonder of the gospel is not the love of the beautiful; it's that Beauty kisses the Beast.

The Beast isn't loved because he has changed; the Beast is changed when he is loved. Joy doesn't come when he's loved for his beauty; joy overwhelms him when he is loved *in his hideousness.*

If the Beast were loved for his beauty, it would be an unbearable burden. Any day he might be scarred, and in any case, soon he will certainly be a wrinkled old man.

So why do we burden our children with the unbearable load of "being good little boys and girls like the heroes in the Bible"? We wouldn't load a pack mule with the burdens we place on our children.

WHY DO WE READ SCRIPTURE, ANYWAY?

Many of us carry within ourselves a default bias when we read Scripture. We think the Bible is about rules for right behavior. Of course Scripture teaches morality; if we are tempted to rob a bank, the Bible has something to say to us. But that isn't its main purpose.

In the Garden of Eden, God gave one rule. It would fit on a Chinese fortune cookie: *Don't eat from that tree.* And we blew it. Do we really think God said to himself, "I know the problem with the Bible so far: it doesn't have enough rules"? If we can't keep one rule, we'll certainly fall short of the Ten Commandments (and the hundreds of others).

God's primary purpose in Scripture is to reveal himself, his love, and his justice. The rules do show how we are to live, but more importantly, they reveal the character of God, and then they show us how far we fall short of it. Our falling short drives us to God's grace—the grace that is revealed on every page of Scripture; the grace that is God's self-revelation; the grace that reveals his purpose in writing the Bible.

THERE'S GOTTA BE A BETTER WAY

Let's teach the wonder of the gospel. Let's show our kids that God loves us ... simply because he loves us. *In our beastliness.* That he loves us *before* we are good. That his love isn't vague sentimentality but cost him his most precious treasure in order to turn us into his prized possession. That the storyline of the Bible is God's search-and-rescue mission to find the dying Beast and kiss him into joyous life.

Let's teach our kids that

- Abraham was an idol worshiper, and God loved him and pursued him;
- Joseph was a narcissistic boy, and God loved him and pursued him;
- David was a murdering adulterer, and God loved him and pursued him; and
- Esther had sex outside of marriage with a non-believer, and God loved her and pursued her.

Our heroes weren't loved because they were good; they became good because they were loved.

We may believe in the innocence of youth, but our children know better. They see the children in the schoolyard (and they see us at home!). They don't need the counterfeit gospel of pack-mule moralism. They need the kiss of the Beauty.

Maybe we do too. After all, it's what the Bible really teaches.

*****

Chapter 2
Why Do Our Children
Leave the Church?

In holy contemplation
We sweetly then pursue
The theme of God's salvation,
And find it ever new.
— William Cowper

Why do so many people—with incredible conversions—parent children who leave Christianity? History overflows with great saints whose offspring lost faith.

- Samuel was a mighty prophet of God. His sons were a mess.
- David was a man after God's own heart. His children were a disaster.

- Harvard, Yale, and Princeton were founded on the gospel. Now they lead the opposition.

I've witnessed dozens of families (and churches, ministries, and prayer groups) who began with a furious fire of love for God but whose next generation couldn't blow a smoke ring.

Our children lose fire because of our mother-of-all-assumptions: we *assume* the gospel. In his book *Marks of the Messenger,*[2] Mack Stiles shows how the gospel is lost:

1. The gospel is *Accepted*
2. The gospel is *Assumed*
3. The gospel is *Confused*
4. The gospel is *Lost*

Stiles continues, "For any generation to lose the gospel is tragic. But the generation that *assumes* the gospel … is most responsible for the loss of the gospel" (emphasis added).

That generation is us. We are most responsible. Who has bewitched us?

WE'RE CONVERTED BY ONE MESSAGE AND WE TEACH ANOTHER

It's 100 percent predictable that we are converted by one message and then preach another. We are converted by the unbelievable hope of God's love for the undeserving, but we lecture on behavior. We all do. Including you and me.

A friend of mine lived wildly until the age of thirty. He slept with scores of women, drank an ocean of beer, and was a self-admitted, abusive jerk. In a desperate time of brokenness, he heard the hope of the gospel and talked with Jesus. He became a pastor.

He was converted by grace, yet his sermons nagged and scolded:

- You should never tell coarse jokes or cuss.
- You should be generous, and that includes making sure you tip 20 percent.
- You should always bring your Bible to church.

Day after day, week after week, he proclaimed the Nike gospel: "Just do it!" We do too.

THE DAMNABLE PRESUMPTION OF ASSUMPTION

One day I asked my friend why his messages concentrated on behavior and not the gospel. He replied, "My congregation knows the gospel. Now they just need to know what to do." He assumed that they understood and embraced the gospel of grace, and then he wondered why his shrinking congregation was so joyless.

My friend's own moral life was empowered by a gospel-fueled heart, but he rebuked and lectured on behavior. In his personal life, he remembered, "What *did* Jesus do?" yet publicly he harangued and scolded with the moral whip of WWJD: "What *would* Jesus do?"

(I sometimes wonder if the first thing Jesus would do is to make a whip of WWJD bracelets and chase the moralists from his sanctuary.)

Martin Luther wrote in his *Commentary on Galatians*, "Continually listen to the gospel that teaches not what I *ought* to do (for that is the job of the law), but what Jesus Christ *has done* for me. This is the gospel. It is the primary article of all Christian truth. It is most necessary that we should know this article well, teach it to others, *and beat it into our heads continually*" (slightly edited; emphasis added).

The gospel is God's love first, our behavior second; moralism simply teaches behavior. The gospel sets God's initiation first, then our response; the heresy of the Pharisee sets our behavior first, then God's response.

We need to beat the gospel into our heads continually. Otherwise, we'll assume it, confuse it, and lose it. And so will our kids.

WHAT FUELS OUR LIVES?

Willpower fuels moralism; the gospel fuels godliness. "What we do" is Pharisaism; "what God did" is gospel.

Willpower hardens: "I straightened out my life, so why can't you?" The gospel softens: "God loved me though I didn't deserve it, so how can I look down on any one else?"

Besides, who gets the glory when our morality increases, us or God?

The gospel is always about God's actions. Even the Ten Commandments begin, "I am the Lord your God, who brought you out of the land of Egypt, out of the house of slavery" (Ex. 20:2). Only after God's action does it command, "You shall have no other gods before me." (v. 3).

Jesus says of the prostitute in Luke 7:47, "She loves much because she was forgiven much," and the apostle John says, "We love because he first loved us" (1 John 4:19). But we forget God's action and moralize, "Don't worship idols, and make sure to show love to your neighbor."

Our kids reject Christianity because they can't distinguish it from mere morality.

HOW DOES A CONSTANT GOSPEL REMINDER CHANGE US?

Time and time again, Scripture (Jesus) says, *Unless you know the why, you'll never be able to do the what.* Unless we have his power, we'll never obey his commands.

What will make us tell the truth when a lie will get us out of trouble? There are only two options: either we harden ourselves with, "Grit your teeth in times of temptation," or we allow the gospel to soften us with, "Jesus promised to be faithful even when we are unfaithful, and he kept his word even though it meant derision, rejection, thorns, and the cross."

Which God will we worship—the god of self-powered moralism or the Lord of all grace?

* * * * *

Chapter 3
Esther: Why Whitewash
God's Scandalous Grace?

*God goes after the prostitutes, tax
collectors, lepers, and sinners. Why?
Because they know they need him. It is
the self-righteous Pharisees, posing in
their own moral goodness, who reject
him.*   — Unknown

W hy do we paint our biblical heroes more hero-
ically than the Bible does? Hiding the faults
of our heroes robs us of grace. That's why the Bible
doesn't hide them.

In chapter 1, I suggested that we tell true stories of
our heroes, stories that show God's pursuit of them despite their failings. I pointed out that...

- Abraham was an idol worshiper, and God loved him and pursued him.
- Joseph was a narcissistic boy, and God loved him and pursued him.
- David was a murdering adulterer, and God loved him and pursued him.
- Esther had sex outside of marriage with a non-believer, and God loved her and pursued her.

When I shared these points in my blog, I was surprised by how many readers were upset by my negative description of "good" Abraham, Joseph, and David. I wondered, have any of those readers even read the stories?

In particular, I was astonished at the hailstorm of angry emails—hundreds of them—from readers who hated my history of Esther. Esther is beloved. Many think she was forced into sexual slavery. I think she was a complicit adulterer. But before you decide to write me an email of your own, hear me out.

WHY WON'T WE ADMIT ANY SHORTCOMINGS IN OUR HEROES?

Let's put aside (for a moment) Esther's willing compliance or innocence. The deeper issue is this: Why do we begin reading the Bible with a built-in bias for its heroes to have an innate goodness?

Nowadays, we want to think of Esther as being pure as the driven snow, but for over two thousand years, readers thought otherwise. When early readers read

Esther, they saw moral ambiguity at best. And like us today, they did not like it.

- The first translations into Greek added words to "improve" Esther's character, saying she never violated kosher law and she abhorred the bed of the Gentile.[3]
- For the first seven hundred years of the Christian church no one—not one person—wrote a commentary on Esther.
- Luther wrote, "I am such a great enemy of the book of Esther that I wish it hadn't come to us, for it has too many heathen unnaturalities" (slightly edited).

We are biased. We want Esther and other heroes to be *naturally* good because we misunderstand the evil within ourselves, and we fail to grasp grace. Instead, we grasp for high self-esteem and believe God primarily works with inherently good people.

Like us.

HOW WOULD A PERSON WHO FEELS BROKEN RECEIVE ESTHER?

A woman called me shortly after my villainous questioning of Esther's purity. She had been raped as a sixteen-year-old by an uncle. She spent the next ten years using her body to gain men's affection, and even occasionally for their money. She said,

> When my uncle raped me, it was mostly the force of his personality, but there was a tiny bit of me that was complicit. I didn't resist,

partly because I wanted the attention of any man who at least wanted something I had. In subsequent encounters [with the uncle], I even took the initiative.

Now [over twenty years later] I understand the brokenness of that little girl who was abandoned by her father; I understand the innocent longing for affirmation; I feel for that little me who was confused and without tools to cope.

But I still felt guilty for the little part of me that participated. I thought, *God could never use me.* Then I read Esther and understood that God can make even the smallest into something great. The story of Esther brings me hope.

This woman's uncle was monstrous. He was guilty of an abominable exploitation of a young woman's confusion. I sympathize with her confusion, and I love the comfort she receives from Esther.

It is this woman's *brokenness* that allows her to see and draw hope from Esther's brokenness. Conversely, those who feel they possess an innate goodness refuse to see God's heart-changing grace.

(Note: It is common for abused children—and later in life, their adult selves—to feel guilty, as if the abuse was their fault. Guilt feelings do not necessarily equate to real guilt. Those who have experienced such childhood trauma were abused by monsters. I do not want to imply, even in the tiniest way, that the fault was somehow that of the children. The guilt rests entirely with the perpetrator.)

Does God use us because we are born good? Or does God take the most broken—even the most brutalized—and turn us into "possible gods and goddesses that if others saw now, they would be strongly tempted to worship" (C. S. Lewis, slightly edited)?

Where will God receive the most glory: in the natural strength of our intrinsic goodness or through the majesty of his supernatural, transforming grace?

SO WHAT ABOUT ESTHER?

Esther lived in an age of brutality beyond imagining. Hundreds of girls were taken for the king's harem. Perhaps some saw it as an opportunity, but many must have hated it. (The age was also brutal to men. Every year, five hundred boys were taken captive and castrated to serve as eunuchs in the Persian court [Herodotus 3.92].)

Scripture never mentions Esther's inner life. It only describes her behavior. It says neither "She wanted to be queen" nor "She loathed the idea." It only describes her behavior. And what is that behavior?

- Scripture commends Daniel for identifying as a Jew and not defiling himself with unclean food. Esther eats all the food provided.
- Shadrach, Meshach, and Abednego resist their king's command under threat of a fiery death. Es-

ther pleases her king more than all the other virgins of the harem.

- Ezra condemns any Jew who marries a Gentile. Esther loses her virginity in the bed of an uncircumcised Gentile whom she marries only later, and she is crowned queen.

Some say that Esther had no choice; others say she should have resisted to the point of death. Some even say suicide was preferable to allowing that defilement.

HOW WOULD I HAVE DONE?

Far, far worse than Esther. As a kid, I used to wish I had been one of the disciples so I could have been the lone friend who didn't abandon Jesus. As an adult, I know myself better.

I admire the bravery of the disciples—not, of course, their "bravery" during the crucifixion but their courage in detailing their faults in the Gospels. The Gospels overflow with the disciples' ambition, stupidity, and cowardice. Sharing such candid accounts took guts. Why do you think the gospel writers were so transparent?

SOMETHING CHANGED IN ESTHER

Esther's predecessor, Queen Vashti, was banished for defying the king. Esther won the king's favor by *not* defying him. Yet the book climaxes when she finally *does* defy him.

In making her decision, she exclaims, "If I perish, I perish." It reminds me of the three men standing before Nebuchadnezzar's fiery furnace who said to the king, "Our God can save us. But even if he doesn't ..."

WHY DO WE WANT OUR HEROES TO HAVE BEEN SO GOOD?

Karen Jobes wrote a terrific commentary on Esther. She says, "Other than Jesus, even the godliest people of the Bible were flawed, often confused, and sometime outright disobedient. We are no different."[4]

Let's not falsely disparage biblical characters, but let's not ignore their failures either. Because we are just like them: flawed, confused, outright disobedient, and proud.

Why do we want our heroes to be better than they really are? Because we think *we* are better than we really are. We would see more of God's transforming grace if we spent more time acknowledging our own failures, just like the Bible does with its heroes.

After all, God can raise up inanimate stones to be his righteous ones.

Isn't it more hopeful—and truer to the gospel—that God's miraculous, transforming power is wonderfully displayed for all the world to see when he takes the broken stones that we are, dips us into the furnace of his love, and then draws us back out as nuggets of pure gold?

God can make the littlest great, but he can't use the greatest until we become little.

Chapter 4
Graceless Goodness:
The Problem with Moralism

*It is impossible to get from
preoccupation with behavior to
the gospel. The gospel is not a
message about doing things. It is a
message about being a new creature.*

— Unknown

When I was nine or ten years of age, I hit my sister.
(I'm sure she deserved it.)

My parents were not happy. They sat me on the sofa.
They told me that my behavior was unacceptable. They
asked me if I wanted to be the kind of person who retaliated with violence.

And then they orchestrated unpleasant consequences.

I don't remember the actual consequences of that day, but whatever they were, they worked. I never again retaliated with violence.

But look at the motivations for my morality. My parents appealed to my identity (I didn't want to be *that* kind of person), and they appealed to my comfort (I didn't want to experience *those* kinds of consequences).

In other words, my parents taught me morality by appealing to my self-centeredness.

THE PROBLEM
The problem with the world is that people lie, cheat, and steal. But we lie, cheat, and steal precisely because we are self-centered. Our moral teaching substitutes one form of selfishness (lying, cheating, and stealing) with another (identity and comfort).

We're curing heart disease with cancer, and the cancer is bound to metastasize. Someday our well-nourished selfishness will no longer be offset by selfish identity or comfort; then we'll lie, cheat, or steal. After all, we've been taught to act in selfishness.

Scripture promises that someday the Law will be "written on our hearts" (Jer. 31:33). God doesn't merely mean we'll memorize the Law. He means we'll have changed hearts. Someday we'll avoid violence because we love others, not just because we fear the consequences.

Let me show you how God performed such a heart transplant in an Old Testament prophet.

THE CURIOUS CASE OF JONAH'S HEART

Jonah's story is famous because of the "whale thing." Instead of the whale, let's look at Jonah's heart. In his story, there is a seesaw activity between God's Voice and his Orchestration. Eventually we see a change in the desires of Jonah's heart.

His story begins with a Voice: "Jonah, go to Nineveh and preach" (Jon. 1:2 par). Jonah disobeys and flees. So God Orchestrates a consequence, the whale.

The Voice comes a second time, and this time Jonah obeys and goes to Nineveh. But his heart is not yet changed. He preaches the world's least loving sermon: "You're all going to burn, and I'm going to roast marshmallows" (Jon. 3:4—okay, that was paraphrased a bit too).

God acts through Jonah's sermon despite Jonah's graceless heart. The prophet doesn't even offer the option of repentance—yet, despite his oversight, the Ninevites repent of their evil and violence (Jon. 3:5–8).

God relents of his judgment, and Jonah is mad. (What, no judgment of those nasty people!) God then Orchestrates a plant to grow, and it comforts Jonah from the heat. Then God Orchestrates for the comfort to disappear. And Jonah gets even madder.

Finally God's Voice speaks one last time: "You have compassion for a mere plant, but you did nothing to

make it grow, and it came and went in a day …. Should
I not have compassion on … 120,000 people who do
not even know their right hand from their left?" (Jon.
4:10–11 par)

This time Jonah's heart melts. The Law is finally
written on it.

HOW DO WE KNOW?

How can we know Jonah's heart is changed? Because
the book of Jonah was written—by Jonah.

In it, Jonah describes his own weakness and sinfulness. He confesses his disobedience; he describes his
own bigotry and hatred of the Ninevites; he shows his
desire that they receive punishment, not mercy; he expresses his anger at God for showing mercy; and he
confesses his own selfish pettiness at the loss of the
plant.

Only a changed heart can do that. The story of Jonah
is the story of a man confessing his self-righteousness.
Prior to God's Voice and Orchestrations, Jonah could
easily have prayed, "Lord, thank you that I'm not like
those evil Ninevites" (Luke 18:11 par). Afterward, Jonah would have prayed, "Lord, have mercy on me, a
sinner" (Luke 18:13 par).

Jonah's story is the story of a moral but self-righteous
man needing God's mercy.

GOD IS AFTER OUR HEARTS

The final words in the book of Jonah are, "Shouldn't I [God] have compassion on ... 120,000 people who do not even know their right hand from their left?" Clearly God is pursuing Jonah's heart. God isn't satisfied with Jonah's external (even selfish) obedience. God wants Jonah's heart to be changed.

The unwritten final question in the book of Jonah is, what will *we* do with *our* hearts? Will we be the selfish, self-righteous Pharisee who prays, "Thank you, Lord, that I'm not like these other sinners?"

Or will we be like the man with a tender heart who prays, "Lord, have mercy on me a sinner?"

Chapter 5
The False Gospel
of "Just Do It"

*The church has spent so much time
inculcating in us the fear of making
mistakes that she has made us like
ill-taught piano students; we play our
songs but we never really hear them
because our main concern is not to
make music but to avoid some flub
that will get us in dutch.... I have
now heard the strains of grace, and
I grieve for my friends who have not.*
— Philip Yancey

A year or so ago, a Christian friend described how
he was beginning to bring the gospel to his softball

team. He had joined the local league that spring—partly for the fun of the game and partly to meet non-believers outside his Christian bubble.

However, he felt uncomfortable with his teammates' cussing during the game. He asked them if they would stop, at least while he was with them.

They agreed and stopped (for the most part). He deemed this "cleaner language" an evangelistic victory. It hinted that his teammates might be choosing the right path.

He felt that somehow the gospel had been advanced. Next he planned to ask them to stop drinking.

Something about my friend's story felt discordant. I didn't sense anyone closer to God.

Somehow, I felt the gospel had been perverted.

BUT I WASN'T EXACTLY SURE WHY

The world is filled with brokenness and oppression. We should be men and women who fight for justice and love our neighbor as ourselves. But that activity isn't the gospel.

Linking the cessation of cussing to introducing the gospel unsettled me. It was like a slightly off-key singer or a slightly out-of-tune instrument. The soft dissonance of my friend's story continued to disturb me. I couldn't shake it. But I wasn't quite sure why.

Then I heard someone critique the modern version of the gospel. He said the modern gospel is:

Sin less. Work harder. Give more.

And that's just wrong. It is a counterfeit gospel, and counterfeits succeed only when they look like the real thing. The problem with the false gospel portrayed above is that everyone smitten by the gospel *will* sin less, and *will* work harder, and *will* give more.

It's just not the gospel. Morality is a result of the gospel, but it isn't the gospel.

IT'S ALSO NOT JUST A MODERN COUNTERFEIT

I've asked dozens of people, both believers and non-believers, who the greatest enemies of Jesus were. Virtually everyone says the same thing: the enemies of Jesus were the Pharisees and scribes—the religious leaders of the day.

No one—not one—answered that the enemies of Jesus were the tax collectors, the prostitutes, or the adulterers (or the cussers).

Isn't that weird? People of all religions—even non-religious people—consider Jesus to be a great moral teacher. Yet his greatest enemies were the moralists, and some of his best friends were society's sinners. It seems upside down. Wouldn't a moral teacher's friends be the moralists and his enemies be the sinners?

When asked by Pharisees about his upside down living, Jesus answered, "Healthy people don't need a doctor—the sick do. . . . I came to call not those who think they are righteous, but those who know they are sinners" (Matt. 9:12–13 par).

Jesus didn't say that the Pharisees were healthy and the tax collectors were sick. He said—in effect—that the tax collectors *knew* they were sick while the Pharisees, in their arrogance, mistakenly thought themselves healthy.

Someone is going to say I'm against morality. I'm not. I wish everyone in the world were a thousand times more moral, including you and me. But in our morality, we need to be cautious. Sound moral behavior apart from the gospel can lead us—ever so slowly—to feel good about ourselves, which can lead us—ever so slowly—to self-righteousness. Which is the enemy of the gospel.

Another counterfeit gospel is "Hey, I'm not so bad. I'm okay, you're okay." It's a modern version of the ancient Pharisee. We don't see our need. And such self-righteousness is killing the world.

The key difference between the sinners and Pharisees was that the sinners knew they were needy.

IDENTIFYING COUNTERFEITS

One way the Secret Service trains its agents to spot counterfeit money is to spend lots of time handling genuine currency. The best way to spot a counterfeit is to know the real thing.

So, what is the real gospel?

- The gospel is not us being good so God will like us; it is God loving us despite our brokenness and sin. All we really need is need.
- The gospel is not us showing God our good report card; it is Jesus living a perfect life and giving us his good report card as our own. All we need is need.

- The gospel is not us emptying our bank accounts to give to God; it is God pouring out his riches on us, the morally bankrupt, to make us rich. All we need is need.
- The gospel is not us cleaning up our acts or our families or our relationships or our mouths; it is God cleaning them up for us. All we need is need.

Tim Keller says that the gospel is like a two-sided coin: we are more wicked than we have ever dared admit, and we are more loved than we ever dared imagine.

Or, we were in such a dreadful moral condition that the death of the Son of God was our only cure, and his love for us was so great that he died "for the joy set before him"—and that joy is us.

When we admit that we are needy—in desperate need of a heart transformation—then the receipt of unearned love for us changes us. His love gives us the needed transformation.

When we can admit that we are really no better than anyone else *and* that we are also incredibly loved, then—and only then—will we be able to love those around us who don't live up to our moral standards.

Because, like others, we didn't live up to them either. But God loved us anyway. So now we can comfort others with the comfort we've been given.

Even when they cuss.

* * * * *

Chapter 6
The Temptations of
Christian Publishing

While the apostle Paul was not
antinomian, he was very close to it. ...
That brings me to a syllogism with two
premises and a conclusion. Premise:
The real Christian faith is close to
antinomianism. Premise: A lot of
modern day Christianity is not at all
close to antinomianism. Conclusion:
A lot of modern day Christianity is not
real Christianity.   — Steve Brown

A few weeks ago I was driving home from a re-
treat with a friend who has five terrific kids and

a great—almost fairytale—family life. His kids seem to smile as they obey.

I admired his parenting skills and asked him his secret. He admitted his desire to write a parenting book. It would address issues such as

- Kids, cell phones, and when
- Television, video games, and limits
- Daily chores, responsibility, and allowance
- Older kids, younger kids, care, and leadership

My friend is bright, articulate, and humorous. I said his book would sell hundreds of thousands of copies. And then I added—it just slipped out—

"And you'll doom millions of kids and their parents to hell."

It was after midnight, I was tired, we were hours from home, and it just slipped out. And of course my friend's teaching will doom neither kids nor their parents. But my slip of the tongue sure stimulated a great discussion.

Besides, *In vino veritas*; and sometimes, in long drives late at night with tired friends, we discover a hint of truth as well.

LET ME EXPLAIN

My friend knows the grace of God. Yet his prescription for parenting was a bullet list of "wise" to-dos. His list was excellent, but it missed our deepest need: walking with God. His list reminded me of the Pharisees.

Despite their bad rap, the Pharisees began well. Their name—meaning "one who is separated"—reflected their desire to be free from impurity. They fought against assimilation into the surrounding pagan culture by creating a religious culture.

They were the sages who taught the Bible in local synagogues. They sympathized with the common people, and they opposed the elitism of the priestly class. In their struggle to nurture a pure culture, they created hundreds of "wise" rules for right living.

Over time, their rules obscured the intent of the Law. The sheer volume of regulations created a culture of external compliance, forgetting that God looks on the heart.

The Pharisaical sages began with good intent and ended as whitewashed tombs.

THE DAMNING PRESUMPTION OF ASSUMPTION

My friend embraces the gospel, but he assumed his readers would too. So he skipped past the gospel and jumped to action items. It reminded me of how the gospel is lost (from chapter 2):

- The gospel is *Accepted.*
- The gospel is *Assumed.*
- The gospel is *Confused.*
- The gospel is *Lost.*[5]

This is the evangelical world: we began with the Spirit and end with a to-do list. We accept the gospel, assume others do too, and then we talk about performance.

The *assumption* of the gospel leads to *confusion* about the gospel: Is the Christian life a daily conversation with God, or is it the Nike commercial: "Just Do It"?

Like the Pharisees, we wash the outside of the cup with our doing. But Jesus says, "First clean the inside of the cup ... and then the outside will be clean as well" (Matt. 23:26 par).

MODERN CHRISTIAN PUBLISHING HAS MUCH TO ANSWER FOR

Rabbinic sages scoured the Scriptures and summarized them with 613 dos and don'ts.

On a whim, I once scoured the websites of Christian publishers. I stopped when I had "summarized" over 1,500 dos and don'ts for wise Christian living:

- *Seven Steps to a Better Christian Marriage*
- *Ten Rules for Right Parenting*
- *Twenty Ways to Love Your Neighbor*
- *The Three-Month Plan for Controlling Your Finances*

All these titles are fictitious, but they represent thousands—thousands!—of real titles.

I fear many Christian publishers are the modern, paid scribes (literally) of "Just Do It"-based Pharisaism. Are we selling our gospel birthright for a bowl of financial gruel?

IT'S NOT JUST THE LEGALISTS WHO DO THIS

I have another friend who *has* written a book. This friend knows the gospel personally. He talks about it, he blogs about it, and I think he lives it. But after his book was published, he wrote a dozen blog posts about topics in his book. They were all behavior-oriented.

- He wrote about how we need to listen before we speak.
- He said we each need to learn to take adventures.
- He suggested that we must begin to be ourselves and not try to be someone else.
- He told us to take time with our kids and spend less time at the office.

I agree with everything he suggests. And these aren't in the legalist's list (don't smoke, don't dance, don't cuss, and make sure you tithe). But, somehow in some way, they still feel like he is just giving us another set of good behaviors.

All of them are good, but more than them, we need the gospel of grace.

SO WHAT DO WE DO?

The tips and techniques of Christian tutors aren't bad, but they obscure the intent of the Law. They encourage *Little Engine That Could* thinking—"I think I can, I think I can"—instead of driving us to God as we realize, "I'm pretty sure I can't."

The Law is not first and foremost rules for right living, though many of us approach it that way. The Law, first and foremost, is a verbal painting of the beauty of God. It is only the reality of God that will change our hearts. More than rules, we need God. And with God, and with a God-changed heart, we begin to live aright; the Law is written on our hearts.

When Jesus expounded on the Law about adultery (Matt. 5:27–28), he didn't offer "Five Steps to Safeguard Your Marriage." He was saying, "You've already committed adultery in your heart. You don't need new rules; you need a new heart. You need God because you can't self-create a new heart."

The book of Hosea is the autobiography of a man who buys back his incredibly unfaithful wife at a great cost and then woos her back with great love. Similarly, the life of Jesus demonstrates a God who ransoms back his adulterous people at incredible cost and then woos us back with unbelievable love.

Our greatest need is not more wise techniques. Our greatest need is to see, know, and walk with God. It's only seeing the reality of God ransoming and wooing us that will change us.

It is not in doing that we see God; it is in seeing God that we begin to do.

MY ASPIRING AUTHOR FRIEND

I asked my friend how he and his wife developed their great list of parenting skills. He said that whenever they encounter a new issue, such as when to give cell phones to kids, they take time to seek God, hear his voice, and examine how God has fathered them.

I told him to write *that* book, and I'll be first in line to buy it: *How God the Father Is Parenting Me, and How He Changed My Parenting Forever.*

I hope that book sells millions.

Chapter 7
The Ugliness of Religious Righteousness

There was already a deep black wordless conviction in his heart because he saw that the best way to avoid Jesus was to avoid sin. — Flannery O'Conner

Hurricane Sandy was the second most devastating hurricane in United States history. On October 29, 2012, it stormed ashore in New Jersey, leaving a wide wake of destruction.

But the destructive path was random and arbitrary. Huge clusters of homes were annihilated while houses right next door were unscathed.

A week after the hurricane, I saw a post on Facebook. It showed the picture of a man standing in front of his unharmed house. Next to it, the scattered remains of his neighbor's house lay completely destroyed by the storm. Under the picture was this caption:

> The Lord's curse is on the house of the
> wicked,
> but he blesses the dwelling of the righteous
> (Prov. 3:33).

I never met the man and I don't know his heart. I hope his insensitivity was simple naiveté and that his judgment of his neighbor was unintentional.

But it smacked of smugness. It reminded me of the ugliness of religious righteousness.

WHY IS IT UGLY?

Religious righteousness is self-righteousness with a dash of religion. It oozes the arrogance of inner self-goodness as it scorns the evils of the less fortunate; it takes credit for personal success while it altogether forgets grace.

True kingdom living nurtures humility: "I can't do it on my own—even be good." And if I can't do "it" on my own, how can I despise anyone else who also can't?

Verses like "God blesses the righteous" are *prescriptions* for hope in God's power; they are not *diagnoses* of our own moral greatness. When we use external circumstances to quantify our goodness, we snub others with our superiority.

Or if the circumstances are negative, we despair. I personally know real believers who have experienced terrible losses:

- A man who lost his son to a brain tumor
- A woman who lost her husband in a freak accident
- A friend stricken with a congenital nerve disorder

Did they lose their son, husband, or health because of their wickedness while you and I prosper because of our goodness? Were they faithless while you and I were faithful?

When we use such verses as self-congratulations, we are insensitive, mean, and ugly. Jesus said, "[God] causes his sun to rise on the evil and the good, and sends rain on the righteous and the unrighteous" (Matt. 5:45 NIV).

Maybe our good circumstances have nothing to do with our goodness. Maybe they're just God's mercy.

LET'S STRIVE TO BE GOOD

The Law tells us to strive for godly character, and the modern world doesn't like it. It smacks of moralism. But the world is filled with violence, oppression, brutality, and treachery. It suffers because people do not strive for goodness.

We should teach, preach, cajole, and encourage everyone to live morally, full of goodness.

But it won't be enough.

THE OVERLOOKED POINT OF THE LAW

Our feel-good, therapeutic view of the world—I'm Okay, You're Okay—will dislike the second purpose of the Law even more than the first. First the Law tells us how we are supposed to live, and then it tells us how we can't do it on our own. Luther wrote,

> The Law is a mirror to show people what they are like ... The foolish idea that a person can be holy [or righteous or good] by oneself denies God the pleasure of saving sinners.

> God must therefore first take the sledge-hammer of the Law in his fists and smash the beast of self-righteousness and its brood of self-confidence, self-wisdom, self-righteousness, and self-help.

> When the conscience has been thoroughly frightened by the Law it welcomes the Gospel of grace with its message of a Savior who came ... to preach glad tidings to the poor, to heal the broken-hearted, and to grant forgiveness of sins.[6]

Few people will seriously admit their own contribution to the evils in the world. (I'm told that Hitler thought himself a pretty good guy.) Using the Law as a mirror to reveal our inadequacies will drive us to God for his grace. If that mirror simply makes us humbler, then the world will be a better place.

THE BEAUTY OF GOSPEL RIGHTEOUSNESS

Tim Keller often says, "Jesus came to live the life we should have lived and to die the death we should have died." Jesus didn't come to earth just to die for us. He also came to live for us.

That means Jesus perfectly lived a life of love, holiness, obedience, and righteousness. In his righteousness, though, he didn't snub us. Instead, he poured out his goodness into us. When God looks at us, he literally sees the goodness and righteousness of Jesus.

Therefore we can stand confidently in righteousness. Yet we stand humbly because our righteousness isn't self-righteousness. Even righteousness is a gift, and that gift is the law of grace.

If grace rules, all circumstances can bring peace. If our house escapes the next storm, we rest in Christ's righteousness. If our house is flattened in the storm, through the resurrection we know that God brings the greatest joys out of the darkest nights.

It's all grace.

* * * * *

Chapter 8
The Insidious Danger of
"I'd Never Do That"

Hi, my name is Jack Miller. I'm a
recovering Pharisee. — Jack Miller

I used to work for a company that created software for publishers. It handled mail orders that were accompanied by checks, cash, or credit card information.

We had a balancing tool that ensured all the money that came into the mailroom was entered into the system and deposited in the bank. It protected against embezzlement.

In 1988, we installed the software at a large Christian publisher. When management heard of our checks and balances, they were appalled. They felt it questioned the integrity of their employees. They asked us to turn off the balancing feature.

A year later, a timid, gray-haired, rooster-pecked grandmother—a long-term employee of the publisher—stole fifteen thousand dollars.

Afterward I asked her, "Why?" She shyly stammered, "It was so easy. The money was just sitting there. It was just so darn easy." She added, "I'd heard of embezzlers before. I always said, '*I'd never do that.*' And then I did."

HER SIMPLE PATH TO SELF-DESTRUCTION

This simple grandmother's self-identity of "I'd never do that" led to a false self-confidence, but when external constraints were removed ("It was so easy"), she became a thief. Her self-pretense allowed a weed of greed to grow in her heart.

How many weeds grow in our own hearts, secretly nourished in the soil of "I'd never do that"? How many of us secretly think, But I'd never [take your pick] ...

    use drugs

    be unfaithful

    cheat on my taxes

    molest a child

    resort to violence

We see others divorce or commit adultery. We may even have been betrayed by one of them. We say, "I'd never do that." But can we be sure? If we had that person's parents, *their* lives, *their* temptations—and if we had *their* restraints removed—do we honestly know what we'd do?

If God removed those same restraints in our own lives, might we do the very same thing? Or maybe something different but equally harmful or even worse?

WHAT IF ...

What do we mean when we say, "I'd never do that"? Do we mean "I *would* never do that" or "I *could* never do that"? I think we tell ourselves "I would never" when what we really mean is "I could never."

But what if we could? What if, for one sliver of time, God looked away; what if we knew that no one—not even God—would ever find out; and what if we knew that even our conscience would leave us alone this one time? Do we know what we might do?

This is actually the terror of the Ring of Power in J. R. R. Tolkien's classic Lord of the Rings trilogy. Given the Ring of Power sought by the evil sorcerer, Sauron,

- Galadriel would become "great and terrible. ... All shall love me and despair."
- Boromir would save his people from Sauron by becoming an evil substitute.
- In the end even Frodo yields to the Ring's irresistible temptation. He is saved by an external force—Gollum's teeth.

Granted the same unlimited power that the Ring represents, with every restraint removed, perhaps we would not do the evil that Sauron did, but we might do something else equally awful.

GOD'S GRACE IN RULES AND RESTRAINTS

Restraints such as accountability groups, peer pressure, or willpower temporarily save us from destructive behavior. We agree to them in moments of clarity to strengthen us in moments of confusion.

Restraints are like training wheels. They keep us upright as we develop an inner poise. But in a moment of mechanical failure, the wheels may fall off and we crash.

How dare we disparage our friends when their training wheels break! Our friends may actually have more inner poise than we do—just not enough to stay upright on their own. It is God's grace, not our personal greatness, that keeps us from falling.

Is our claim, "I'd never do that," a heart-numbing mantra we chant to keep us from looking to grace?

THE DANGER OF RULES AND RESTRAINTS

Moralism is not the proliferation of rules and restraints. The multitude of regulations are simply symptoms, training wheels for our training wheels. Moralism itself is self-assurance based on right behavior that arises from external restraints.

But God desires a changed heart, not training wheels for our training wheels. When we rest our hearts on our restrained behavior, we are in a moment of grave danger.

A time will come—and it will!—when external restraints disappear or our willpower is exhausted.

What will we do then?

If our heart rests on "I'd never do that," we will fall, and great will be that fall. But if our hearts rest on "There, but for the grace of God, go I," (found in God-given restraints and God-formed inner poise), we will ride upright in freedom. And great will be that ride.

WE NEED A STRENGTHENED HEART

God wants inner strength of heart, not just external restraints. He says, "Do not be like the horse or the mule ... held in check by bit and bridle" (Ps. 32:9 par).

Almost any restraints that keep us from trampling on each other are good, and we should seek them and use them. But let us remember that those bits and bridles are simply training tools that teach us to rely on God's grace; they are meant to support us as our hearts are reshaped with his desires.

Someday the bits and bridles are coming off. Our kids' training wheels are too.

Retrained behavior is good, but a Spirit-changed heart is better. Only God himself can strengthen our hearts. Not rules or restraints. Only a relationship.

HOLDING ON TO GOD

I haven't spoken to the woman who embezzled since that interview twenty-five years ago. I don't know where she is today, or what she is doing, or whether she is even still alive. But I'll always remember how she concluded our discussion.

"Sam," she said, "I used to go church because I thought, 'I'd never do that.' Now I'm holding on to God for dear life, because I know I might."

Chapter 9
Why Can't We Admit
the Evil Within?

*The gospel is this: I am more wicked
than I ever dared admit, and I am
more loved than ever I dared dream.*
                              — Tim Keller

A few months ago a woman told me about her inner life. She said she is growing in a sense of her own sinfulness.

- Her thought life, she admitted, is more judgmental than it should be.
- Her good deeds, she acknowledged, are partly motivated by self-congratulations.
- Her repentance, she confessed, is often shallow.

Now, as far as I can tell, this woman is not committing adultery, nor is she robbing banks (at least not recently), nor is she kidnapping children for the sex-trade industry. I don't think she lies much either.

Yet she claims a growing sense of her own badness while at the same time experiencing a greater joy in her relationship with God.

This wicked-joyful woman is my eighty-seven-year-old mother.

WHO ARE THE REAL OPPRESSORS?

Day after day I hear a chorus, like an annoying advertising jingle I can't rid my mind of, singing the self-serving lyrics, "I'm a good person; I'm a good chap; I'm just not so bad."

When we read history or simply look around us, which people are the ones who oppress, coerce, and tyrannize? Is it the humble or the arrogant?

- Is it those who claim, "I deserve what I have and probably deserve what you have too," or is it those who admit, "I don't even deserve the little I have"?
- Is it the ones who proclaim, "I worked by the sweat of my brow; what's your problem?" or is it those who confess, "I don't deserve a fraction of what I have, so you can have some of it as well"?

It is a documented fact that the poor in the world share more generously than the rich. That's because they know that the little they have is a gift. Their kind of wisdom has a name: it's called *humility*.

I DON'T CARE WHAT OTHERS THINK OF ME

Pop culture croons an eerie cliché:

I don't care what others think of me; I only care what *I* think of me.

It sounds like freedom. The opinions and agendas of others no longer control us. That's good. But think with me a moment.

Does it comfort us to claim our high jump bar is so low that we can trip over it and still win the blue ribbon?

There's a term for people unmoved by the opinions of others, who lack shame or guilt, who are caught up in a false sense of their own value. We call them sociopaths.

WE NEED TO KNOW WE MATTER

One desire drives every human soul: we need to know that we matter. This drive is alive because we are made in God's image. His image in us is significant. And so are we.

The need for significance drives the desperate, non-stick nature of our consciences to deny our failings. We say, "I'm a good person." We deny our badness because we're frantic to claim our value.

But failure to admit the evil in us actually prevents us from knowing our value. The truth—which is inside out, upside down, and contrary to common sense—is that we will find our deepest value only when we admit our deepest failings. It's a paradox, yet it's the only way to find value.

THE PREACHING WE HEAR HASN'T HELPED

Many of us have been punished from the pulpit and tortured by talks of our failings: "You're wicked; you have nothing to offer; you are of no value." Conviction without grace kills our hearts. And it totally ignores our intrinsic worth. We are made in the image of God, and we have something good to offer to the world.

Others of us have been pampered from the pulpit and therapized by talks: "You are good, shame is bad, God is love, and everything is groovy." But there's no electricity. God loves me; sure, what else is new? Love without cost isn't grace. And it isn't life-changing.

Instead, we need the paradoxical preaching that proclaims, "We are worse than we ever dared admit, and we are more loved than we ever dared dream." The only love that will move us is the love that costs, the love that swam the deepest ocean to restore us.

WHAT IF SOMEONE ELSE'S OPINION DOES MATTER?

Let's say you're a cello player and you say, "I don't care what others think. I only care what I think." How much satisfaction will you get? How much will your self-proclamation warm your heart?

But what if Yo-Yo Ma (perhaps the greatest living cellist) magically appeared at your recital and exclaimed, "That was unbelievably beautiful and artistic!" Your soul would soar with significance, and your heart would blaze with fire.

The opinions of others *do* matter. It just depends on who the other person is.

THE MOST GRACIOUS WAS
THE MOST CONVICTING

Jesus described the Law more strictly than anyone before. He said we are adulterers if we simply harbor lustful thoughts. He said we are murderers if we call others a fool. How could gracious Jesus make the Law so harsh and still remain so full of grace?

He did it out of mercy to drive us to him so we could see our utter need of him. We need to know the evil in us *and* his love, both at the same time. It's the only path to humility without hopelessness and confidence without arrogance.

The best significance is given. We either receive it freely from the grace of Jesus ...

OR WE CAN JUST GRAB FOR
IT BY OURSELVES

Last week my wicked-joyful eighty-seven-year-old mother bumped into a family friend who stocks shelves at a department store, a young woman with Asperger's. The two chatted as my mother waited in line.

When they got to the head of the line, the cashier said to the young woman with Asperger's, "Why are you always annoying people? Get back to your shelves."

My stunned (and wicked and joyful) mother paused, looked at the cashier, and whispered, "You know, that was a cruel thing to say."

The clerk, grabbing for self-significance, replied, "Hey, I'm a good person. I have a good heart."

Our path to the high mountain of joyful assurance passes through the valley of humble self-admission. Grace is called grace because it is a free gift that is undeserved.

Chapter 10
When Willpower Runs Out

*The moralistic gospel may fill our
churches with well-behaved people. But
the result will merely be an improved
version of the old man—not the new
man that the biblical gospel promises.
Without grace, we miss out on true life
transformation.... Grace accomplishes
what moralism promises but can never
deliver: a changed heart.* — Trevin Wax

A man I know refuses to ask himself, Why? When
sexual temptations entice, he grits his teeth and
orders himself, Resist! When other people irritate him,
he furrows his brow and wills himself, Be nice. When
anxious feelings rear their heads, he decapitates them
with a hearty, Begone!

But the thing is—and I'm not sure how to phrase this—he seems arrogant. He handles life so very well; what's wrong with the rest of us? His advice to sufferers is, "Don't do it," "Be happy," "Suck it up," or "Just stop!"

If I'm ever hurting … well, his number is not on my speed-dial.

Another man I know came to me a year ago because someone told him he complains too much. He asked me what I thought.

The truth was, he *did* complain a lot. Grumbling seemed like the bass-drum beat of his conversational style: "My wife is a slob," "My boss it too demanding," "My colleagues are unappreciative," and "No one wants to talk with me."

Yikes! I wasn't sure how to answer him, but I uneasily admitted that he might grumble more than most. I asked him why. He left in a huff, determined never to complain again (though I've wondered since if he complained to his wife about me).

A few months later he was no longer complaining. He was angry—livid with his wife about her housekeeping, angry at his boss about an assignment, and furious with coworkers for their ingratitude. He had exchanged self-pitying complaints for other-blaming fury.

It was not an improvement.

WE NEED TO RECOGNIZE A
SPIRITUAL PRINCIPLE

External "sins" arise from inner forces. There is a stimulus *beneath* the sin. Our constant complaining, anxiety, and frustration are the result of inner pressures on the heart. Willful repression of external sin does nothing to relieve that inner pressure.

Until we deal with it, the pressure will find an escape in other forms. Whining yields to rage, lust gives birth to lethargy, and gluttony nourishes greed. Treating the symptoms instead of the cause is like putting a Band-Aid on a broken arm.

BESIDES, WILLPOWER RUNS OUT

Each of us is born with a natural reservoir of resolve. Our self-control takes various forms. Some endure crying babies for hours while others control their tempers for years; some have physical stamina while others have seemingly limitless patience with people.

But our willpower is only *seemingly* limitless. My tank may hold ten gallons and your tank may hold twenty, but empty is empty for everyone.

What do we do when our supposedly inexhaustible self-discipline is exhausted?

We explode. Oh, we explode in different ways. Some actually *implode* and sulk in self-pity. Others blow up in a blast of rage and resentment. Some freeze up with paralyzing anxiety, and others cheat on their spouse, drink themselves blind, or swindle their partners. But however it manifests, the explosion is never pretty and always destructive—often to those around us and always to ourselves.

REPETITION AND HABITS OF THE HEART
Repetition is a tool that creates instinctive behavior. Musicians practice scales and tennis players practice serves. Over time, muscle memory causes such people to act instinctively, and that's good. Usually.

Long-term appeal to willpower also creates instinctive behavior: self-reliance based on personal resolve. No matter how good our short-term behavior may be, the instinct we cultivate over the long term is to rely on ourselves. The habit of our heart is personal will.

But what happens when that resolve runs out? The rains fall, the rivers rise, the winds blow, and the house built on sand falls. Because willpower is an exhaustible resource.

There is another way. We can let our sin drive us to God.

Contrary to all that we think or feel or have been taught, sin can be an invitation to intimacy with Christ. We may believe that we need to clean up our act in order to come to God, but that's exactly backwards; the truth is, we can't clean up our act *until* we come to God.

Each of us engages various prayer triggers, Morning-time devotions; Mealtime prayer; Stress-time intercession. Let's create another trigger: Temptation-time Why?

"Lord, *why* is this temptation so appealing? What is going on in me beneath the surface? What inner longing am I trying to satisfy that only you can fulfill?"

It may seem upside down, but sin is an invitation to intimacy with God.

A NEW HABIT OF THE HEART

Scriptures insist that "unless the Lord builds the house, the laborer's work is useless" (Ps. 127:1 par), but our hearts habitually act on their own. We say to God, "Just give me the blueprints," and then we grit our teeth, furrow our brow, and start laying brick.

God didn't come to earth to give us more moral blueprints or doctrinal design plans. He shed his blood to make us friends, co-laborers in his construction project. God wants friends, not independent contractors.

Going to God with the whys of our lives builds moment-by-moment conversation.

This is not navel-gazing; it is God-gazing. This is not self-focus; it is conversation with the Creator. This is not psycho-babble; it is a visit with the world's greatest healer.

LET'S CHOOSE DOOR NUMBER THREE

Self-reliance on willpower has only two results: misery when we fail or smugness when we succeed. Despair drags others down with us; pride drives others down under us.

There is a third door. When tempted to ridicule a friend or rob a bank, let's resist! But let's not rest in our weak resistance. Let's pound on the doors of heaven and ask, "Why? What deep pressure on my heart makes this temptation so attractive?"

As we go to God in our emptiness, God fills us with his grace. As we cry to God when our willpower runs dry, he empowers us with a Spirit-changed heart.

Chapter 11
We Read the Bible
the Wrong Way

*We come to Scripture not to learn
a subject but to steep ourselves in a
person.*   — C. S. Lewis

Have you ever been in a relationship in which everything you said was misunderstood? Communicating in such circumstances can drive you crazy. It's as if the other person has a built-in bias to misinterpret you.

• You say their new tie is attractive. They wonder if you are buttering them up in order to borrow fifty bucks.

- You privately mention that their plaid pink tie clashes (in the tiniest way) with their striped orange shirt. They think you are a critical jerk.
- You say nothing at all about their new tie. They figure you are a self-obsessed narcissist who never notices anything about anyone else.

A built-in-bias prevents such a person from hearing what *you* have to say because their hearing is filtered through their own agenda. They only hear what their faulty translator allows them to hear. They only hear what they are conditioned to hear.

Guess what: *We* are that biased, agenda-driven person, only it's what God says that we misinterpret. We read Scripture through the lens of *our* purposes, and we overlook *his* purpose.

We are missing the boat to a rich life with God and boarding a dinghy to relational hell.

THE MISREAD PURPOSES

Our personalities and training bias us to read Scripture through one of these three lenses:

- *Doctrinal.* We primarily read Scripture as a handbook for how to think. Francis Schaeffer, a leading twentieth-century Christian thinker, claimed that his biggest temptation was not temptations of sensuality but temptations toward abstract theological truths. Thinking-oriented people see the Bible this way.

- *Behavioral*. We primarily read Scripture as a guide-book on how to act. We see the Bible as God's guidelines for human behavior. It is about the right and wrong of actions. Legalistically oriented people read Scripture this way.
- *Inspirational*. We primarily read Scripture as a manual of inspiration. The normal course of human life brings difficulties which result in pain. We just feel bad. We read the Bible as an emotional supplement to bolster our feelings. Feeling-oriented people read scripture this way.

Please don't misunderstand me (and, by the way, that is a very nice tie you are wearing). It is only in Scripture that we discover true doctrines, right behavior, and great inspiration. But none of these are the primary purpose of Scripture. These misinterpretations thrive because they are so close to the real purpose. The best counterfeits are the ones closest to the real thing. They just aren't it.

SO WHAT IS THE BIBLE ALL ABOUT, ANYWAY?

On the road to Emmaus, Jesus meets two doctrinally weak, behaviorally confused, emotionally depressed disciples. He challenges their truth, changes their behavior, and brings them joy. How does he do this? He reviews the Scriptures and explains that the Bible is all about him: "Beginning with Moses and all the Prophets, Jesus interpreted to them in all the Scriptures the things concerning himself" (Luke 24:27).

Jesus says, "All of Scripture is about me." The Bible is a self-portrait painted by God.

Scripture is God's revelation about himself. *The Bible is not about us!* It is about God. It's not about our pet doctrines, personal behaviors, or feel-good inspirations. First and foremost, the Bible is God's self-revelation. He's showing us who he is.

Until we understand that the Bible is about God, we are lost when we read it.

SEEING JESUS

Jesus claims that abundant life lies simply in knowing Jesus (John 17:3). It's knowing a person. It's not dogma, behavior, or mere inspirational feelings. C. S. Lewis said, "We come to Scripture not to learn a subject but to steep ourselves in a person."

The four Gospels are obviously about Jesus. They're filled with his birth, life, death, and resurrection. But can we really "see Jesus" in other places such as the Law, or proverbs, or stories of early heroes? After all, Jesus said that *all* Scripture is about him.

ARE THE PSALMS ABOUT US?

We can easily see Jesus in a few messianic Psalms. He is the Supreme King (Ps. 2, 45, 72) and he is the Suffering Servant (Ps. 28, 55, 102). But what about all those other "normal" Psalms, like these verses from Psalm 71:4–5:

"Rescue me, O my God, from the hand of the wicked, from the grasp of the unjust and cruel man. For you, O Lord, are my hope, my trust, O Lord, from my youth."

At first, these verses are inspiring. We ask for God's protection from injustice. We cry out that he is our hope and trust. From our youth. The verses seem to be about us.

But wait a minute. I merely *want* him to be my hope and trust, but the truth is ... well, I'm really not so hot at making him my hope. Instead I place my trust in my ideas and street smarts. There is no one—not one saint, male or female—in the history of the world who has fully placed their hope and trust in God. Every human has failed.

EXCEPT ONE

Only Jesus really placed his hope and trust in God, and Jesus did it when he was in the hands of the wicked and in the grasp of the unjust. Only Jesus trusted from his youth. Not you nor me.

In this Psalm (and all the rest), when we are honest, we merely see our failure. This Psalm cannot be about us. If it is, what hope do we have? Because we fail all the time.

But Jesus did more than die for us: *He also gave the life he lived to us.* When God looks at us, he sees a person (Jesus) putting all his hope in God in the time of his deepest darkness. If we read the Psalms with Jesus in mind and understand that his beauty has been given to us, we have no need to despair over our weakness.

When we see Jesus in Scripture, we see perfect truth, righteous living, and inspired communion with God; but now it is personal and no longer abstract.

LET'S LOOK AT OLD TESTAMENT CHARACTERS

Sure, some Old Testament characters are types of Jesus, but can we see Jesus everywhere?

- Jesus is the *true* brother Abel, innocently slain, whose blood cries out for our acquittal, not our condemnation.
- Jesus is the *better* Abraham who answered the call of God to leave the comfort of the familiar and go out into the world.
- He is the *real* Jacob who wrestled with God and took the blow of justice we deserved so that we—like Jacob—only receive the wounds of grace to wake us up.
- Jesus is the true and better Moses who stands in the gap between the people and the Lord and who mediates a new covenant.
- He is the better Job, the only truly innocent sufferer who intercedes for his friends.
- He is the better David, whose victory over Goliath becomes his people's victory, though we never lifted a stone to accomplish that victory ourselves.

- He is the true and better Esther who said, "*When* I perish, I perish."
- He is the true Jonah who goes into the belly of hell itself so the people could be saved.[7]

TRY AN EXPERIMENT WITH ME

Try to see the person of Jesus in your Scripture study. Or do the following:

- Try reading the story of Joseph and ask God to reveal Jesus to you (Gen. 37, 39–45, 47).
- Read Psalm 56, see that it is about Jesus, and recognize the gift of Jesus' life to you.
- Look at the parable of the Good Samaritan and try to find Jesus in it (Luke 10:29–37).

Seeing the heart of Jesus in all of Scripture brings the peace we desperately need. Our hope doesn't depend on how good we've been. Let's be honest: we screw up every day. Our hope depends on seeing Jesus.

*****

Chapter 12
If Grace Is True, Why Be Moral?

Pride is the ruthless, sleepless, unsmiling concentration on self.
— C. S. Lewis

The nature of sin is not immorality and wrongdoing, but the nature of self-realization which leads us to say, "I am my own god." This nature may exhibit itself in proper morality or in improper immorality, but it always has a common basis—my claim to my right to myself.
— Oswald Chambers

I once talked with a group of college students, and one of them asked, "How do you explain Westboro Baptist? I can't stand Christianity because of churches like them."

Have you heard of Westboro? They picket military funerals in protests against gays. Their website is *God Hates Fags dot com* (I can't bring myself to type the link).

Westboro Baptist is a tiny church. Where they fail to attract many members, they excel at attracting the media. And where they fail to represent the true church, they excel at representing what's wrong with the church.

I've never met a soul from Westboro, and I've never met anyone who's met someone from Westboro, and I cannot say anything about any of its members' hearts.

But I can say this: if we don't understand churches like Westboro, we'll never understand grace.

WHY DO WE DO THE THINGS WE DO?

Everything we do is driven by a motivation. In the Western world—where a McDonalds is on every other corner—unimportant actions (like eating French fries) are driven by trivial motivations (like a hankering for McCarbs). But every action of consequence is driven by a dominant, heart-absorbing motivation: We need to know that we matter. We long for significance; we have to be special.

Our personalities differ, and our solutions for significance differ as well. That is why our lives, our decisions, and the groups we join are so incredibly varied.

But underlying our different choices lies one unifying drive: we need to know we're significant.

- Some crave power and use every fiber of their being to dominate, often ruthlessly oppressing others to grasp for control.
- Romantics long for love, and you'll find them flitting from one affair to the next, betraying one lover when they find someone more satisfying.
- The greedy think wealth will mean they matter, and they cold-bloodedly seek money, even cheating and betraying friends to seize it.

Finally, many get their significance by being good. These people flock to our churches.

IT'S NOT EVERY CHURCH MEMBER, BUT ...

Jesus said that the church would be filled with *wheat* and *weeds* (Matt.13:24–30). We suspect that those hypocritical weeds are the adulterers and thieves hidden among us, and we think the wheat are the good people. Like us.

But Jesus says that many of the "weeds" actually do good deeds:

> On judgment day many will say, "Lord, didn't we prophesy in your name, drive out demons in your name, and perform tons of miracles in your name?" I will tell them clearly, "I never knew you. Get away from me" (Matt. 7:22–23 par).

Paul suggests much the same thing when he writes,

> If I have enough faith to move mountains,
> but lack love, I'm nothing. If I give away
> every penny I have, and even if I surrender
> my body to be burned, but lack love, I gain
> nothing (1 Cor. 13:2–3 par).

Doubtless, some church weeds are those wicked sinners we imagine, but many of the weeds are those moral people who preach, heal, give away tons of money, and even die for the faith.

Are we scared yet? We should be.

HOW CAN THIS BE?

Every evil in the world comes from self-centeredness and our constant crusade for self-significance. So dominators rape, the greedy pillage, and the love-hungry lust. We "ruthlessly, ceaselessly, unsmilingly concentrate on ourselves" (C. S. Lewis, paraphrased).

And if our self-significance comes from being a good person, we ruthlessly and unsmilingly join a church, the place where morality is praised.

Evil deeds are motivated by self-centeredness, but so are many good deeds.

SELF-APPLAUSE

Jeremiah 9:23 describes it this way: "Let not the wise man praise himself for his wisdom, let not the mighty man praise himself for his might, and let not the rich man praise himself for his riches" (slightly paraphrased). We normally hear this passage read using the word *boast*, but the literal meaning of the Hebrew is "*hallelu* himself" or "praise himself."

We could add self-righteousness to Jeremiah's list. When Isaiah says that all our good deeds are as filthy rags (Is. 64:6), he could just as easily have told us, "Let not the good man praise himself for his goodness."

We desperately crave significance; we are driven to know we matter; so we save ourselves with self-applause through our wealth, wisdom, and strength. And our goodness.

WHAT ARE WE TO DO?

Every evil deed by every single human has been triggered by our self-centered solutions for satisfying our longing for significance. The conundrum is that we *are* made for significance. We *are* made to matter. It's in our DNA. We are made in the image of God.

Our longing for significance isn't the problem. The problem is our self-saving solutions for self-applause—in both the wicked and the moralist. The only solution that will work (and the only solution that will heal the world) is the right praise from the right person.

Paul exclaimed, "God forbid that I should boast except in the cross of our Lord Jesus Christ" (Gal. 6:14 NKJV). The solution to our need for significance is to boast—to get the strength of our hearts—from the applause of the right person: "At that time each one will receive his praise from God" (1 Cor. 4:5 par).

WHAT DOES IT MEAN TO BE A CHRISTIAN?

Being a Christian is more than believing that Jesus is God's Son; Satan knows that too. It's also more than being a good person, which may only be our own moralistic efforts at self-saving. And it's more than the magical claim that we have a good heart—because if we have one, why doesn't it show?

Being a Christian means that our self-saving died with Christ—that old person who self-applauded through self-significant deeds is buried six feet deep.

It means that we have risen to a new life where all the significance we'll ever need is lavishly poured into us—even though we didn't deserve it—thanks to the self-sacrifice of Jesus, who died *for the joy* of having us as his brothers and sisters.

Being a Christian means that we finally cease from the interminable striving for self-applause, and we rest by faith in the significance freely given to us by God's grace.

SO WHAT DOES ALL OF THIS HAVE TO DO WITH BEING MORAL?

Our immorality (and morality) used to come from grasping for self-significance. When we finally have the only significance in the world that will satisfy, something changes.

What does grace have to do with morality? Everything.

- When we're tempted to lie to save our reputation, we now have the only reputation that will really satisfy us: we are the beloved of God.
- When we're tempted to control others for self-glory, we now have the only glory that will ever fulfill us: we are praised by God.
- When we're tempted to steal, we now have the only wealth in the world that will content us: we ourselves have become the treasure of Christ.

How does Westboro Baptist help us understand grace? By using it as a mirror, we see ourselves clutching and clawing, grasping and gnawing for self-significance, whether through immoral hatred or self-serving goodness. And we turn to the free gift of grace.

What about driving our kids to be like those heroes of the faith from chapter 1? Let's look in the mirror of our ceaseless striving and see that our battle to have the best kids in town may be a symptom of our self-serving significance to be the best parents in town.

The real heroism of those heroes we hold up as behavioral models for our children was when those heroes recognized their own inadequacy and rested in grace, the freely given love and applause from God.

Jeremiah closes his passage above with this: "Let him who praises himself praise himself for this, that he understands and knows me" (Jer. 9:24 par).

And by grace we finally do know him: Jesus, the only truly Good person ever. Grace means we now do good deeds for Goodness' sake, no longer for our own.

＊＊＊＊＊

Afterword

Despite its title, this book is not about Sunday school or its teachers. It's about our daily need to remember grace. If we want heart-changed joy and heart-changed morality, we need grace.

I had the good fortune to sit under many gospel-oriented Sunday school teachers. They constantly reminded me that God doesn't love me because I'm good, but that I can literally become good as I rest in God's love. The wonder of the gospel isn't love of the beautiful; it's that Beauty kisses the beast.

Thank you, my Sunday school teachers of long ago, and thank you modern-day Sunday school teachers, the thousands of you who faithfully teach the gospel week after week and year after year. You shall receive your praise from God (1 Cor. 4:5).

How do we teach little children the scandalous chapters of our heroes of the faith? I don't have a general principle, but I still remember what my third or fourth grade Sunday school teacher, Mr. Tappen, taught me.

He said that King David, even though he was married, began kissing and dating another woman. I was shocked. I still feel the visceral punch at David's act of betrayal. Mr. Tappen never mentioned adultery—I doubt I even knew what sex was at that age—but he successfully communicated the shame of infidelity.

And then Mr. Tappen taught us about David's repentance in Psalm 51. I only remember what he said about the first verse, but I've never forgotten his insight. The verse reads, "Have mercy on me, O God, according to your steadfast love; according to your abundant mercy, blot out my transgressions."

Mr. Tappen asked us to notice the reasons that David asks for forgiveness. David didn't say, "Forgive me according to how bad I feel," or, "Forgive me because I'll try really hard in the future." David simply asked God to forgive him because of, and according to, the measure of God's immeasurable love.

That's why it's called grace.

Sam

Endnotes

1. Tim Keller, "Changing the City with the Gospel Takes a Movement," posted September 3, 2012, in *The Gospel Coalition* blog, *http://thegospelcoalition.org/blogs/tgc/2012/09/03/changing-the-city-with-the-gospel-takes-a-movement/*.

2. Mack Stiles, *Marks of the Messenger: Knowing, Living, and Speaking the Gospel* (Downers Grove, IL: InterVarsity, 2010), 40.

3. Greek translations of Esther add six long "chapters" which scholars identify by letters A through F (to distinguish them from the Hebrew chapters that we number). Section C:26 adds, *"[God,] you know I abhor the bed of the uncircumcised,"* and C:28 adds, *"[I] have not eaten with them at their table."* See this translation of the Greek additions: http://ccat.sas.upenn.edu/nets/edition/17-esther-nets.pdf

4. Karen Jobes, *Esther, The NIV Application Commentary Series* (Grand Rapids: Zondervan, 1999).

5. Stiles, *Marks of the Messenger,* 40.

6. Martin Luther, *Commentary on the Epistle to the Galatians,* trans. Theodore Graebner, Kindle Edition, Location 1675, slightly edited for modern language.

7. I heard most of this list in a doctor of ministry course by Tim Keller called *Preaching Christ in a Postmodern World.* I cannot recommend this course highly enough, and it's free on iTunes.

About the Author

S am Williamson is the son of a pastor, the grand-son of missionaries, a speaker, a writer, and—he hopes—a *thought-provocateur*. He studied European intellectual history at the University of Michigan.

Finding no jobs in European intellectual history, he spent twenty-five years in the mundane business of business, the last two decades as an executive and own-er of a software company.

After his twenty-five year stint in business, he felt called to ministry. He founded *Beliefs of the Heart*. Its mission is to help us examine the unexplored convic-tions that drive us. Why do we do what we do? What unseen forces motivate us? What is going on beneath the surface?

Sam and his wife, Carla, live in Ann Arbor, Michi-gan, and have four grown children and an ever increas-ing number of grandchildren. In his free time he loves sailing, skiing, and scuba diving.

Read more of his writings—or subscribe to his weekly articles—at **www.BeliefsoftheHeart.com.** You can contact him at: Sam@BeliefsoftheHeart.com.

Made in the USA
Columbia, SC
29 May 2019